GRANNY SMITH Was Not an Apple

THE STORY OF ORCHARDIST MARIA ANN SMITH

Written by Sarah Glenn Fortson

Illustrated by Kris Aro McLeod

PETER PAUPER PRESS, INC.
Rye Brook, New York

To Beth who always requests Granny Smith apples be added to her
Cream of Wheat and to Dylan, Stephanie, and Bryan.
I love you all so much. —Sarah

For Miler, with love —Kris

Text copyright © 2023 by Sarah Glenn Fortson
Illustrations copyright © 2023 by Kris Aro McLeod

Library of Congress Cataloging-in-Publication Data

Names: Fortson, Sarah Glenn, author. | McLeod, Kris Aro, illustrator.
Title: Granny Smith was not an apple : the story of orchardist Maria Ann Smith / written by Sarah Glenn Fortson ; illustrated by Kris Aro McLeod.

Other titles: Story of orchardist Maria Ann Smith
Description: First edition. | Rye Brook, New York : Peter Pauper Press,
  Inc., 2023. | Includes bibliographical references. | Audience: Ages 4-8
  | Audience: Grades K-1 | Summary: "In the 1800s a migrant farmer named Maria Ann Smith worked as an apple orchardist. Her discovery of a new type of apple
that never turned red, but was always green, tart, sweet, and perfect for a pie, was due part to a fluke of nature, and part to Maria's insight and determination.
The beloved Granny Smith apple that we know today was named in her honor. This is her story"-- Provided by publisher.
Identifiers: LCCN 2023018237 | ISBN 9781441339447 (hardcover)
Subjects: LCSH: Smith, Granny, 1799-1870--Juvenile literature. | Applegrowers--Australia--Ryde (N.S.W.)--Biography--Juvenile literature. |
Apples--Growth--Juvenile literature. | Apples--Varieties--Juvenile literature.
Classification: LCC SB363.2.A8 F67 2023 | DDC
  634/.1109944--dc23/eng/20230504
LC record available at https://lccn.loc.gov/2023018237

Published by Peter Pauper Press, Inc.
3 International Drive
Rye Brook, NY 10573 USA

ISBN 978-1-4413-3944-7
Printed in China

7 6 5 4 3 2 1

Visit us at www.peterpauper.com

Author Acknowledgements

I would like to thank the following people: Angela Phippen, Local Studies Librarian, City of Ryde, Australia; The Mitcham family at Hillside Orchards in Tiger, Georgia
Kris Aro McLeod for her beautiful illustrations; and of course, my wonderful editor at Peter Pauper Press, Mara Conlon.

Selected Bibliography

• Museums of History NSW. State Archives Collection. Records. Lady Nugent 27 Nov 1838. *www.mhnsw.au/collections*
• Dahlen, Hannah. "Granny Smith, Not Just about Apples." *Pregnancy, Birth and Beyond.* October 19, 2012.
• Karlstrom, Amanda—Plant Breeder and Geneticist. NIAB (Plant Science and Breeding UK)
• Martell, Nevin. "Sweet, Tart, Crunchy: How to Engineer A Better Apple." *NPR.* October 9, 2013.
• Martin, Megan. "Smith, Maria Ann (1799-1870)." *Australian Dictionary of Biography, Supplement,* 2005.
• Short, Brian. *Apples & Orchards in Sussex.* Lewes: Action in Rural Sussex, 2012.
• Spurway, John. Martin, Megan. "Granny Smith: Who Was Granny Smith?" *City of Ryde.* 1992

Listen carefully.
Do you hear a crunching sound?
Peel back England's fog.
You see Maria Ann Smith.
A woman raised tough to the core.

The crunching you hear is the sound of
her footsteps on the crushed pebble road.
Maria Ann is a traveler.

Walking from farm to farm,
orchard to orchard,
she asks for work.

She will plow or pick or prune.
She will shear or shuck or shell.

Maria Ann is not smiling, because farmers have new machines* that work faster than she can by hand. It's harder and harder to find work.

*A mechanical reaper was one of the machines developed in the 1800s that had a big impact on farming. Seen here is one of the early horse-drawn designs created by Patrick Bell of Scotland in 1826. Laborers using a sickle to cut grains (like the one Maria has) could cut about 1 acre of wheat per day, while Bell's mechanical reaper could cut about 1 acre per hour!

Soon Maria Ann and her husband will not have enough money to care for their family. Their children are looking pale and thin.

Maria Ann helps women in the village deliver their babies.
The women call her *Granny** and pay her with bread, cheese, or clothes.

*A person who helps deliver babies at home
is called a midwife. Historically, midwives
were sometimes called "Granny."

At last Maria Ann finds work in an apple orchard. She learns about harvesting apples and the special process to grow them called grafting.*

*Orchardists do not grow their apple trees by planting seeds because apple seeds do not grow into the exact same apple. And those grown from seeds are often mushy or tasteless. They must use grafting to grow the apples that they want.

First, Maria Ann cuts a piece of branch from a tree that has fruit that she wants to grow more of.

Next, she chooses a root base or rootstock and cuts a small notch in it.

Then she tucks the branch, or branches, into the rootstock and ties them together.

If she does this in very early spring, a new tree will grow by autumn and eventually bear the fruit she wants.

One day, two strangers appear at the orchard. They have come
all the way from Australia,* looking for hardworking laborers who
know about planting, pruning, and grafting. They promise work
with a free voyage to Australia.

Australia

*In the 1800's Australia was
a British colony. At first,
England shipped prisoners there.
Prisoners were used as laborers
to build the towns, but they
were not skilled at farming.
Agents from Australia came
to England to find farm laborers.
They offered to pay for their
passage and to have a job waiting
for them when they arrived.*

Neighbors warn Maria Ann not to go. They have heard rumored stories of seasickness, shipwrecks, and seafaring pirates. Ignoring their warnings, she and her family board the ship to Australia.*

Crossing the ocean takes four months. Her children are sick,
but the thought of a better life keeps her spirits up.

*A passenger list shows that Thomas Smith,
his wife, and five children, sailed to Australia
on the ship, Lady Nugent, *arriving on
the 27th of November, 1838.

On wobbly legs, feeling like she's still at sea, Maria Ann and her family walk off the ship. Her husband and son find the wagon that has been sent for them.

As they lurch forward, Maria Ann hears the familiar
sound of crunching pebbles under the wheels.
She lets out a sigh, glad to be on land again.
She knows about working the land.

Hoping that one day she and Thomas might give their family a home of their own, Maria Ann works long hours in the orchard. She works as a midwife in the village.

She scrimps and saves. Until one day . . .

. . . husband and son are climbing a ladder
    to place a beam
        to give the roof its pitch.

Maria Ann is mixing the mud
    to make the mortar
        to hold the walls in placc.

She scrimps and saves. Until one day . . .

. . . Maria Ann is clearing the land

to plow the rows

to plant the seedlings

to grow the apple trees.

Years later, her orchard is ready. Maria's red apples sell fast at the bustling market. At the end of the day another vendor offers her a box of French crab apples from Tasmania. "Put a few in your apple pies for a bit of tartness," he says.

Before she leaves, she shops for sugar, cinnamon, and nutmeg.
With the spices in her pocket, Maria Ann climbs in her
wagon and turns the horses toward home.

Hours later, covered in flour dust, Maria Ann lines up her steaming pies on the window ledges.

She carries the leftover red apple and crab apple cores and scraps up to the creek bank at the edge of the orchard and dumps them in a pile.

Winter passes and then it is spring. Maria Ann takes a walk through her orchard. When she reaches the creek bank, she glances down and sees a seedling tree growing from the old scrap pile. There's something different about it. The leaves appear to be crab apple leaves.

She nurtures the little seedling over several years—watering and watching. When it finally blossoms, Maria Ann is happy to see bees flitting in and out of the small flowers.

Years later, after the blossoms fall, she finds three green apples. She waits for them to develop at least a bit of red coloring, but they stay completely green. Maria Ann is disappointed, but curious.

She takes one of the green apples to the pump and washes it. She carries it to her kitchen where she peels and slices it.

Gingerly, Maria Ann nibbles at the corner of a slice. Smiling, she finishes it off. The apple tastes like her pies, sweet, but tart.

She asks two neighboring orchardists to inspect the tree and the green apples.
The other orchardists agree. A new apple—perfect and always green—
has grown from the crab apple seedling that Maria Ann has cared
for and the bees have pollinated.*

*Once an apple or crab apple tree blossoms, it must cross-pollinate with different apple or crab apple trees in order to bear fruit. Bees are the main pollinators for apple and crab apple trees.

Early the next spring Maria Ann takes cuttings from the
new apple tree and grafts each to a different rootstock.

Listen carefully. Do you hear a crunching sound?
Peel back the branches and you will see . . .

. . . a gray-haired lady walking between two rows of trees heavy with green apples.

The crunching sound is Granny Smith—biting into one of the
green apples that will soon be named in her honor.

• TIMELINE •

1799   Mr. and Mrs. Sherwood have a baby girl. They name her Maria Ann.
(Maria Ann's parents were also traveling laborers.)

1800   Maria Ann Sherwood is baptized on January 5 at St. Peter and Paul Church
Peasmarsh, Sussex, England. The church still stands today.

1819   On August 8, Maria Ann Sherwood marries Thomas Smith (a farm laborer).
Both the bride and the groom sign the marriage certificate with an "X."

1838   On November 27, Maria and Thomas arrive in Australia on the ship,
Lady Nugent. With them are their five surviving children: Thomas age 16,
Stephen 13, Charles 8, Sarah 6, and another Maria Ann aged 1.

1842   Their last child, a son, William is baptized at St. Anne's Church in Ryde, Australia.

1855-56   The Smiths purchase 24 acres of land in Ryde, Australia. They build a home
and plant an orchard.

1868   Two fruit growers are invited to view an apple seedling growing by a creek.
Maria Ann tells them the seedling developed from remains of Tasmanian crab apples.

1870   On March 9, Maria Ann Smith dies at age 71. She is buried in the cemetery at
St. Anne's churchyard, Ryde, Australia.

1924   An article is published in June in the *Farmer and Settler* by Herbert Rumsey
describing the discovery of the Granny Smith apple. He interviewed the younger
of the two fruit growers who visited Granny's orchard in 1868. The article is considered
the earliest and most authoritative account.

• Note to Parents, Caretakers, and Educators •

While the focus of this book is on the life of Maria Ann Smith and her journey to becoming an orchardist in Australia and cultivating what we now know as the Granny Smith apple, it should also be noted that Maria and her family arrived in Australia as part of the British colonization of the land—a period which had a devastating impact on the Indigenous communities that had already been living on the land for thousands of years. Numbers vary, but it is estimated that 750,000 Indigenous peoples were living in Australia before Europeans arrived. And as a result of conflicts and disease (brought from Europe) the Indigenous population, over the time period from 1788 to 1900, decreased by almost 90 percent. The Australian government has in place a reconciliation plan that includes, but is not limited to, race relations, equality and equity, institutional integrity, unity and historical acceptance. As part of the broader reconciliation plan in an effort to educate, increase awareness, and celebrate the history of the Indigenous peoples of Australia, there is a week-long celebration held every year in July—National NAIDOC (National Aborigines and Islanders Day Observance Committee) Week. Learn more by visiting *www.naidoc.org.au*. Aboriginal and Torres Strait Islander peoples are the oldest continuous cultures on Earth. Indigenous communities across Australia work hard to preserve their heritage (including over 150 extant languages), champion their rights, and build a better future.